SOME INTEGRITY

Padraig Regan is the author of two poetry pamphlets: *Delicious* (Lifeboat, 2016) and *Who Seemed Alive & Altogether Real* (Emma Press, 2017). In 2015, they were a recipient of an Eric Gregory Award, and in 2020 they were awarded the Ireland Chair of Poetry Bursary Prize. They hold a PhD on creative-critical and hybridised writing practices in medieval texts and the work of Anne Carson from the Seamus Heaney Centre, Queen's University Belfast, where they were a Ciaran Carson Writing and the City Fellow in 2021. This collection is the recipient of the 2022 Clarissa Luard Prize, awarded by the David Cohen Foundation.

Padraig Regan
Some Integrity

CARCANET POETRY

First published in Great Britain in 2022 by
Carcanet
Alliance House, 30 Cross Street
Manchester, M2 7AQ
www.carcanet.co.uk

A CIP catalogue record for this book is
available from the British Library.

ISBN 978 1 80017 208 1

Book design by Andrew Latimer
\

The publisher acknowledges financial
assistance from Arts Council England.

CONTENTS

'this is this'
Gertrude Stein

SOME INTEGRITY

50ML OF INDIA INK

Opaque, & black as gravity,
the ink is perfectly unlike

the small glass pot
whose shape it occupies

so passively. It is
something's burnt remains

that makes it black.
It is the sticky leavings

of the lac-bug
that makes it shine.

(The name of the lac-bug
has nothing to do

with absence, but means,
in fact, a multitude.)

It performs its tiny fractal
creep through the paper's

knitted capillaries,
& finds itself astounded

with significance. It means
I am not yet dead.

I was not untempted
to leave this blank.

I

(Studies)

THE UNDERSTUDIES

All night some finches have disgraced themselves
by singing their desires through my open window;
I suggest we abolish the tree they're living in.
I have no desire to write about Laika, nor
the greyscale picture of the world she glimpsed
for five hours from a window, which, regrettably
was not left open. I want to write about the brave
& red-haired fox, the little bee, the starlet,
the coal, & the light breeze. I want to write
about Bobik, or the untamed substitute thereof
who ran like a joke around the barracks.
They who were subject to the same diet
of laxatives & jellied protein. It didn't help
that they were all, in temperament, phlegmatic,
& therefore Cancers, or Scorpios, or Pisces, though
the circumstances of their births went unrecorded
in the streets. Their mothers were abolished
because no-one & themselves desired otherwise.
They had seen some stuff & so Oleg Gazenko
thought they could bear to see some more.
I desire to abolish all desires & live
like a monk, divorced from the world.
I desire to be less sublunary. The secret
of their deaths was kept long past the abolition
of the state they died in service of.
It's hard to think Oleg Gazenko was a person
& desired. In 1998, he spoke
of this again; he said 'we did not learn enough'.

PITCHER PLANTS

I loved them, when I was too young
to think of condoms as I saw them
bunched & hanging from the iron
skeleton of the old greenhouse.
Like quicksand they occupied
more space inside my head
than they have come to warrant.
I thought *balloon.* I thought *soft bell*
with a liquid middle. I thought
wet glove for a single finger.
I knew they do what mouths do
but I didn't know the half
of what a mouth could do. & now
I can't decide if I want to live
like this lipped trumpet,
whose only closure is a leaf-thin leaf
that isn't big enough to plug
its open throat, & who accepts
whatever comes its way — the living,
the dead, & all their mixed excretions.
That there is grace in suffering
is not an excuse for suffering.
I know this. I know my jaw
when it aches, I know my teeth.

A MACHINE FOR HARVESTING OLIVES

The limb of a nude umbrella,
a makeshift robot's hand,
a rake that chose to specialise.
We introduce it to the tree
& comb through the branches.
The olives fall onto a tarp
like fat, soft hailstones,
each one its own insistent fact,
a symbol meaning 'olive'.
Some leaves are unavoidable.
A rough barber, says the tree,
it has dragged my children from
their home in my knotted form.
You think I do not know
what happens in the press?
There my children weep & die;
their oily souls are wrung
from the pulp that once
they called their selves. Well,
it would say that, wouldn't it?

REHYDRATING MUSHROOMS

I'm thinking of how mushrooms will haunt a wet log like bulbous ghosts;
of how a mushroom may be considered a travesty of a flower

in the way that a wolf may be a travesty of a grandmother. Personally, I don't
believe in ghosts, but it has been three months since a man was shot

in a street just next to where I live, & now it seems the ghosts are everywhere
in clouds that stay around the fringes of the sky, in a blur in a photograph

when the camera jerked away, in a thumb-print smudge on my glasses-lens.
When I add water the mushrooms swirl like dull confetti. They begin to print

themselves onto the water, their flavour. A week without rain is enough
to set my skin ticking, so when it comes — prefigured by the smell of it

& thunder playing at the edges of earshot — I go out to greet it
in a tracing-paper-thin dress, no tights,

& it falls on my head like a bolt of gauze & in undisclosed locations
bodies seep into the water-table. It is the first Monday of June, 2016.

A ROAST

The chicken is spatchcocked & nothing
like a book, but it lies open & creases
where its spine once was. It imposes

its own urgent presence upon the table.
It gives meaning to the silverware
& crockery, our teeth & the tongues

that lie behind them. There is charcoal
on my fingers & on everything now.
I've been working on a study

of 'The Christ of the Foundations':
the crucifix Saint Teresa carried
from Avila to Arévalo. There is

a smudge of shadow where His ribs
meet His abdomen; His hips
are wider than you would expect.

The chicken is nothing
like a dress, but its fibres fall apart
in response to my attempts to portion it.

There is a scraping of forks on plates,
a clicking of knives.
I've been having trouble with His face.

I've been trying to map the light
that shapes His unmistakable
cheekbones, & it resists.

The buddleia creaks over the back wall
& the moon, for the occasion,
has dressed as the moon.

RISOTTO

Midnight, & my thoughts have turned to starch: how best to break it down,
    part-way,
before my body does the rest. The paper around the garlic like sheets of dry
    skin;

the skin around the onions like paper. I try to stop my thoughts from
    turning
to the bird whose bones I've commandeered & put to use in a way quite
    unintended.

The grains of rice of are short & fat, & as they're tossed in the warm oil,
    turn
translucent at their edges, but keep a kernel of themselves dense white.
    They are like

the spawn of some amphibian. Everything I do, I do to rob them of their
    nature.
It has been a month or more since I have touched another human skin;

I am ok with this. I divest a lemon of its rind; it comes away in filaments,
each one as yellow & minutely curled as saffron threads, which I can't
    afford.

I add the fat I've stolen from some calf I'll never meet. I eat it & I think
I should have added more. I eat it & I think about the moment that it will
    become

not *it* but *I*. & not without regret, I feel this process taking place. I hate
my commitment to making more self to hate. It is not without regret.

MINTY

For as long as it takes a single drop of condensation to roll its path
down the curve of a mojito glass before it's lost in the bare wood of the table,
    everything is held

in its hall of mirrors. Our faces, yes, blown up & stretched grotesquely like
    balloons,
or inverted in a green liqueur like a cartoonist's idea of alien life. But also:

whatever grid of bricks & wood makes up the room we happen to be sitting in
is dilated & wrapped around a single focal-point; whatever portion of the sky
    that happens

to be visible through the window becomes a convex bowl. The weather also
    happens,
as it always does, & passes on, & brings those other places where it falls into
    the orbit of the glass.

It reads the room. It takes things in & what it takes it rearranges on its surface
(or in its core (if they are not the same)) & gives it back for us to read.

So, fish-eyed, myopic, cataracted with dew, a map of a city's erogenous zones
(a patch of grass, a tree that doubled as a lacy umbrella when our shirts were
    already

soaked transparent, a room full of steam, a jacuzzi's silky jets) establishes a fair
    legibility, just,
in this green bulb. A mojito or a mint julep? I suspect it doesn't matter much.

A SNAIL

Imagine the effort it would take to go on living inside a skin
    so barely-there, so thin
you are required to coat yourself in mucus to stop your wet
    interior from leaking out.

It's this that comes to mind when I go into the kitchen & see
    this chalky leaving on the tiles.
It is the graphy in choreo — some creature's slow & frilled
    propulsion across the floor

preserved as kinks & loops, as gradations in the thickness of
    the line. Oh,
I'm almost reluctant to scoop the bastard up in the bowl of a
    spoon & whip it over the fence.

Speranza believed there might be something worth reading
    in the patterns left behind by snails.
She advised to place one on a plate of flour & leave it
    overnight. When you return,

you should find there etched a letter, the initial of the man
    you'll marry.
I've waited long enough. I scrub it off & watch the water, a
    slick of light on the tiles, evaporate.

KATSU IKA ODORI-DON

I know what animates this bunch of tentacles:
it's just the salt in the soy filling the blanks in the dead nerves.

I tell myself this, but as the GIF keeps looping
through the same few frames, the same pattern of flicks & wiggles,

it's difficult to not imagine necromancy, or worse,
the dumb protest of a lump of brain-stem.

At any moment I could stop this wonky, eight-limbed Charleston,
not by eating it but by closing the tab. I tell myself this.

Is it empathy that's stopping me, a sense of duty
to bear witness & attend to the whims of the dead,

no matter how random? Not quite. Maybe it's envy
or aspiration that keeps me watching. But do I envy

the hand that pours the sauce & turns this stump of a squid
into its own erratic puppet, or aspire to be as pliable

as the clump of tissue that receives its grace?
If, as the physician says, the soul weighs twenty-one grams,

it seems important that we find a way
to figure out how much of this is sodium

& therefore how much of us is lost in a fit of crying,
or passed back & forth throughout a night of sex.

It will take perhaps a minute for the last shudders
to peter out & the tentacles to lie still again.

I want to know is it best to wait before you start
the process of dismantling the legs with your chopsticks

& testing each one for its flavour; or is the reciprocity
of your tongue's movements part of the pleasure of the dish?

When the time comes, feel free to keep a limb of mine
& drench it with soy if you feel lonely.

II

(Reproductions)

LIFE DRAWING: JACOB

Your knees are facts,
miraculous,
& full of bones.
Your feet don't prove
that God exists,
but imply it.
Your left elbow
is a question
about muscle
asked in shadow.
Your right is much
the same, rephrased.
You are a tree,
a piece of fruit
or furniture
& none of these.
You are not Keith
or Scott, or Lee.
You are a text
I must translate
from one language
I can only
half read into
a language I
only half speak.
You are a man
standing. You are,
& have become
biography:
my own. Thank you.

POEM FOR BOBBY KENDALL

who does not exist & who is lying on a bed
whose frame is a diorama of swans
advertising their monogamy. Whose robe
would be dangerously sheer if he

or his ass existed. Who is lousy with pearls
& dancing. Whose décor would put to shame
the most libidinous of courting birds.
Who by the candelabra's orange light

is seductive as meringue & pliable as metaphor.
Who maps according to its johns, the city
that does exist beyond the window
of the room he lives his made-up days inside.

O Bobby, the street is a rat's nest of contingency
& neon & steam from the subway grates.
A storm is blousing in from the mad Atlantic
& pitching the world to its own diagonals,

& Bobby, this is the least of our concerns:
the future is as futures often are
just history we haven't memorised
& I cannot say if you survived it.

REMBRANDT'S *SLAUGHTERED OX*

is slick, brown, & almost yellow.
He seems to understand how colours
might invoke a smell, & here
even the wood of the panels & beams
could tell such stories of blood
as his anatomists won't comprehend
for years, stuck — as they are —
with the humours, with their faith
in the liver as the sanguine valve
that keeps the flow of the body in check.
The cow's four legs are drastically stubbed;
its belly yawns like a hessian sack.
It is a question made flesh: at what stage
of disassembly is 'cow' replaced
with brisket, sirloin, flank & rump?

VERMEER'S SUPPER AT EMMAUS

There is the old white jug
& a whisper of glass in front of it.

There is bread with its mottled interior
& the slurred reflections on silverware.

There is a window cut into the whitewashed wall
whose corner rhymes with the folds

of the cloth that hangs from the table
& remembers the cupboard where it was stored.

There is a figure in yellow & another in blue,
& if you dug a biopsy from each, you'd find

the yellow is lead & tin,
the blue is ultramarine.

Which is just as you'd expect.
What's there is there

& people always want what isn't there.
& so, he painted Christ

with His forehead wide & flat below His thinning hair,
His eyes sunk deep into His skull.

He worked for seven months to get it right.
He took six years to learn to get it wrong.

TWO CABINETS

There is a story behind the cabinets.
When I was young enough to climb inside the smaller one

I would. I was no bigger then than the smaller
of two cabinets my granddad helped to lacquer

when he himself was not much bigger than I was.
Not much happened then, & then a lot of things, but none

of this is the story behind the cabinets. No one
told it to me. Instead they'd say

'there is a story behind these cabinets'
through the keyhole whose key was never found.

My granddad hunted rabbits by staging irresistible salads
on large, flat rocks, over-seasoned with pepper

so the rabbit's inquisitive sniffing would make it sneeze
& launch its eggshell skull into the rock.

This is a thing that happened. The cabinets are almost
as beautiful as the trees they used to be,

or so I like to think, having never seen them.
It must have killed my granddad's granddad's horse

to lug those trunks out from the forest, or so
I like to think. It must have crushed their little cart:

I picture the barrel-tops repurposed for its wheels popping off
like Champagne corks. Everything was something,

once. The air inside the cabinet grew small
around me. In those years meat was scarce.

To see the blank white face of truth. To see the huge & pool-sized eyes of a sadder-than-average horse. To see one's life unspool in colour, once, & once in cartoon-toothy black & white. To see a wall of ice, compacted, sharp as the elbows of a well-built man. To see it melt. To see your daughter & your dog, & see their six legs running tandem on the grass. To see the outline of a bear lumber through the snow & think of meat. To see the handsome priest revealed for what he is. To see nothing because the lamps have burned through the last of the rationed kerosene. To see rain falling from a cloudless sky, or at least agree that you have seen rain falling from a cloudless sky. To see your father grow until he swallows God. To see him shrink until he is a fog inside a jar. To see your brother's face & then remember you don't, in fact, have a brother. To see the jar that holds your father break. To see this & see it clearly.

OUR PERSONAL PAPERS

*'If, before a cartoon sequence by Disney, one read and believed the
caption,* There is nothing else, *the film would strike us as horrifically as a
painting by Bacon'*
— John Berger

Sometimes we get lost in the tall grass. It's summer, & the sky
feels like a very thin blanket. The crickets' manic clicking is
symmetrical to the acute geometry of grass, the blades' weird
intersections. A dog barks in the distance & we remember
that somewhere there are still things like chairs & sandwiches.
A little sweat on the forehead reminds us that we are still
inside a skin, & the skin is a kind of tight net, like a fat quarter
of muslin full of curds & hanging over a bowl it can drip it's
chalky, milky fluids in.

*

We have been reading the same book. The author seems very
concerned with our marriages. He lays out our dreams in
alphabetical order. This amuses us. Each of us finds something
different to look forward to & something to be afraid of. For
example, we look forward to assignations with interesting
persons, but we don't want our horses to turn into pigs. We
rarely dream of water except as a backdrop, & this makes our
dreams inconsequential. We enjoy the flying when it works.
It's tough on the thighs but so much fun! We feel a sympathy
with paper. We don't regret the presence of the wires, only the
crushing horizontals of their arrangement.

*

We saw the American soldiers. We saw the destruction of the fleet by the American navy. We see & describe the interior of the body of our dying mother. We see in advance the man whom we will marry. We have seen towns & landscapes before we have ever visited them. We see our fiancé or an intimate friend dying (these are frequent cases). In our own house we hear a voice singing. It is the voice of a friend now in a convent. We go to visit our husband on a distant steamer & our husband receives this visit. We take no interest in pugilism or pugilists. We see, three years in advance, the commission of a crime, down to its smallest details. We watch the corn market. We see a lady arriving in a railway station, her journey having been undertaken quite suddenly.

*

We affect a sensitivity to pollen. To achieve a convincing fake sneeze requires practice & no small measure of flair. You must commit to the convulsion. The trick is to surprise yourself, so don't plan your sneezes in advance. We rub our eyes until they're red & extruded far above the plane of our face. We imagine pollen spores the size of oranges. We expect them to be sticky.

*

These windows make us feel curated. We are unsure what to do in such few dimensions. A frame is just a method to divide the intentional from the accidental. There is too much of us. We open up the window & drape our arms over the sill. We think of windows as the teeth of a house & we judge a house with broken windows as we would a person with missing teeth. We wonder if we can talk about an art of defenestration. We have read, but not understood, the thing about the arrow that never reaches its target.

*

We rip up handfuls of grass & chew it & spit it out. It is our own quaint revenge, to reduce its spiky linearity to cud.

*

Sometimes disbelief is all we have. It is the burned-out negative of hope. All it takes is to tilt our gaze at a certain angle & our belief in what we see snaps like a cracker. We are yet to find the angle that allows us to view the world as a stack of flat sheets, cut to suggest a sense of depth. It is, we presume, the task of a lifetime. When we look at the sky we expect to find a thick reflection of ourselves. We try to move out of our own way to see those other people behind us, no, behind our reflections.

THE *BARBERINI FAUN*: A PARTIAL RECONSTRUCTION

I.

His foot, a hanging
club; his legs,
an educated guess —
& flickering, almost

in their tension.
The oblique angle
of the pelvis & the ribs
(whose presence you don't

for a second, doubt)
is an innovation
equal to the wheel,
crop rotation,

the discovery
of negative numbers.
His right arm, someone
thought better of.

II.

When the Ostrogoths
had only just begun
their year-long siege
on the capital, stone

was stone & useful
for its own hard quiddity

& not the accidental shape
it was coerced into.

Like everyone, he played
his part: he was uprooted
& thrown from the roof
of Hadrian's tomb,

&, as any soldier
would reasonably hope,
he took more limbs
than he donated.

III.

You can still see
where Vincenzo
stuccoed his thigh
to the remnant

of what it imitates;
where Lorenzo & Giuseppe
cobbled a patella
& its hinge

from the riddle
of stones lifted
from Castel Sant'Angelo's
boneyard of a moat.

It is harder to detect
the trauma to his head,
his head like a fig relaxing
in its own decomposition.

IV.

& you can just make out
the nubbed horns
in his hair's
calligraphic nest,

the twisted cord
of his diminutive tail.
He is clean shaven,
flaccid, his one

remodelled foot
is toes & skin & tendon,
un-cloven, un-keratinous.
I'd rather not believe

that he would spend
his waking hours
knee-deep in rape,
despite the evidence.

V.

It is hard to ignore
his femoral curves
which guide the eye towards
his proportionate balls

& — obsequious
as any frame — announce
the significance
of what they wrap around.

& harder to refuse
to read a meaning
into the aleatory fact
of his cock, whose glans

has been snapped off
& must, somewhere, still
exist, worn small
& smooth as an olive.

VI.

Confronted with this
immanent tonnage
taking the shape
of my desires,

there is very little
to prevent me
from inflicting
one more revision

on the disputed
& brutal text
that is his anatomy —
just this suspicion

that if he woke & saw
the way I gazed at him
he would break my neck
as soon as look at me.

III

(Capriccio)

On 12 June 2016, I was sitting in Woodworkers, watching —
through the huge windows at the front of the pub — rain come
down so hard it seemed to pixelate the façade of Benedicts
Hotel on the other side of Bradbury Place. It was only after
a few minutes of watching that I realised the windows were
open and what I had mistaken for glass was, in fact, just air.
I thought about windows: about the fact that when they are
fulfilling their function most successfully is also when we are
most oblivious of their presence, which means, in a sense, that
one of the functions of a window is to impersonate its own
absence. And I thought about glass: about how it is neither,
in physical terms, a solid nor a liquid, lacking the crystalline
structure of a solid, but whose molecules cannot move like
those of a liquid. The term for this is 'amorphous solid',
though 'glassy solid' is an acceptable, if slightly old-fashioned,
alternative.

I was trying to work out if there was potential in thinking
about glass as a queer material, insofar as its physicality
forces us to confront the fact that the categories we receive as
common knowledge — matter as solid, liquid or gas; gender
as male or female; sexuality as gay or straight — are heuristic
at best and cannot account for the true complex variety of
being, and introduces into those systems of categorisation a
disruptive new term defined only in relation to itself, bending
that system around its own material needs. Which led me to
consider if I could push this line of thought a little further
and suggest that glass may be an exemplar of a certain *erotic*
embodiment, a kind of sluttish, self-effacing passivity, and
whether this could help us to imagine new forms of political
agency, not based on assertions of individual self-presence, but
on more circumspect and generous principles of transparency
and reflection.

I thought about this and then I didn't — a bore of noise came crashing down the stairs from the poolroom and caused the whole thought to snap (or evaporate might be a better word, seeing as it has, eventually, condensed on this page). There was a rugby match on, and the upstairs section of the pub was so full of men that an overflow of bodies had accumulated everywhere: in the smoking area out the back, in the toilets, and around the bar of the downstairs room where I was sitting. And these men were performing that particular (I don't use this word accidentally) occupation of space — the broad gestures, the open legs, the shouting — that straight men do to assert not just their own gendered and sexual selves, but also the rights which emanate from their gender and sexuality: to be recognised as the owners of space, on whose caprice the rest of us may be permitted to remain.

§

I had woken up that morning to reports of a mass shooting in Florida. As I went about my day, more details about the scale and nature of the violence filtered through. In the early hours of the morning (between two and five local time) Omar Mateen had killed 49 people and injured 53 others in Pulse Nightclub, Orlando. A few days later, there was a small vigil for the victims at City Hall. There, I met my friend Caitlin, and we hugged and there was something in the way we hugged that felt as though each of us was trying to communicate our own personal reaction to this tragedy — for me, it was an attack on the queer community (the only grouping to which I feel any allegiance); for her, it was the most recent manifestation of an ongoing pattern of gun violence that had marked the life of her country for decades — while also trying to acknowledge that the other's reaction was just as felt and valid. Belfast being a small city with a proportionally small gay community, there were many people there I recognised, including a boy I had been friendly with at school, but hadn't seen much of since. I asked him if his boyfriend was coming and he explained that his boyfriend, who was only semi-out, wouldn't have felt comfortable at such a public event. Under normal circumstances I would have judged him for this, I would have thought that surely his obligation to my one-time friend should have outweighed his sense of shame; but after the shooting, I understood that this reaction was symptomatic only of my own empathetic limitations, and that the closet was, after all, not an anachronism but still an effective tool in our defensive arsenal.

§

But this was then still the future. I moved to the back of the bar in the hope that it might be a little quieter and looked at a photograph on the exposed brick wall: it was an old school photo, wider than it was tall and filled with the grey faces of three-or-four-hundred boys arranged in disorderly rows. I had looked at this photograph many times before I realised that it was from my own school. By my time, the empty space behind them was filled with a squat, rectangular gym which had already aged into only partial use, but the pointed sandstone window frames of the nineteenth century admin block were just as I remembered and the crest embossed on the white mount was the same Lamb of God and Keys of Heaven I had worn on my chest for seven years. These boys would have been old men by the time I had first set foot in the space where they once posed for the camera. Most likely, some of them were dead.

As I looked at the photograph, I noticed a seam running down its middle, which suggested that the panoramic aspect of the image I was looking at was created by stitching together two different exposures. And, as I followed this seam from the grey complexities of clouds above the boys' heads and into the black mass of their uniforms, I noticed that one boy's face had been bisected and he had lost half of himself in the time it took for the photographer to move his camera fifteen feet or so to the right.

And in a way, I empathised with him; or I projected onto him my own occasional desire to slip away from the world and my own embodied presence within it. A desire which, at that moment, I felt acutely; and which I can trace back to the site in which this boy achieved its fulfilment, where I spent my days surrounded by people whose difference from me was enforced (by myself as much as them, I will admit) as an essential factor in the development of identity; by which I mean that I was subjected to the grinding and ordinary cruelty that the effeminate are told we should expect, and through which boys learn the practice of their heterosexuality (more so than through sex, I suspect).

§

Glitch City is a generalized term used by players of the Pokémon games to refer to maps with invalid tile data. [...] Although some aspects of the source map of Glitch City are preserved (such as some tiles), most other attributes are completely changed (such as what is and is not walkable terrain).

— Bulbapedia, the community-driven Pokémon encyclopaedia

§

In the first generation of Pokémon games, it is not difficult to slip outside of the mathematics that dictates that for every entrance there must be an exit and that the two sides of every door must press against each other. By following a complex but easily replicated series of movements, it is possible to trick the game into warping you to a location that does not exist. Because the game must load something on the screen, it scrambles through its memory and comes up with a collage of tiles: grass, pavements, water, windows and bricks are blended together with numerals and scraps of indecipherable text. And all of these visual signifiers are divorced from what they represent. You can move through a Glitch City, but how and where exactly you can move cannot be discerned from the visual content on the screen: you might find yourself walking on water or, ghost-like, through a copse of trees.

It is tempting to think of the glitch as a random occurrence, to use the word to mean something like a destructive miracle. But a glitch is as much a consequence of the rules governing the system in which it happens as is the system's normal functioning; a glitch not a moment when the system is suspended, but a moment when the system shows its freakish, unplanned depths. It shares this quality with, say, a torrential rain shower in the middle of an otherwise sunny June, or the murder of 49 queer people in a nightclub, which, despite its vital specificity, cannot be extricated from the global discursive regime in which our lives are understood to be material for theological and political debate.

§

Though I didn't go out of my way to ignore it, I didn't follow the inquest into the shooting with much attention. I had no interest in Omar Mateen, nor the attempt to reconstitute his movements and motives from the destructive traces he had left. If I wanted to, I could make an ethic of this: I could say that my responsibility as a writer is not to theorise or explicate violence, but only to attest to its unassimilable presence (and there is a chance I could convince myself to believe this). A year or so after the event, I was talking to a friend about my ideas for this essay, and he told me that the evidence pointed towards the likely interpretation that Mateen was not motivated by homophobia in any direct way, and had chosen

Pulse as the theatre of his brutal display not because it was gay club but because his planned target was closed for the night. I didn't know what to do with this information: both in the sense that I couldn't work out if and how it changed the piece I was working on, and in the sense that I couldn't understand my own reaction to hearing it. I think, at first, I hated my friend for telling me. I got the feeling that my friend expected it to be somehow comforting to learn that the shooting was only accidentally the biggest loss of queer lives in a single incident for more than fifty years, but (although I am sure this wasn't his intention) what I heard was my friend trying to circumscribe my reaction to the violence, to delegitimise my way of understanding the massacre through a specifically queer lens. As I've thought this through, I've come to the realisation that my initial disinterest in Mateen and his motives was, at least in part, valid. The content of his mind as he carried out the attack (as much as this can be made comprehensible) is not necessarily a significant factor in the *meaning* of the event. What gives the event its meaning are the 49 people he killed, their memory and their continuous absence, and, yes, the interpretation of the event in the consciousness of the queer community (at least in those parts of the world where we had become complacent) as a reminder that our bodily safety is, at best, still partial, unequally distributed and dependent on the permission of cisgender heterosexuals, which they reserve the right to rescind.

§

The Gameboy screen I spent a significant portion of my childhood staring at as I explored the geography of Kanto is a two-inch square made up of a film of liquid crystals laminated with polarising glass. It is capable only of straight lines and right angles which can be manipulated into jagged curves, and everything it displays is rendered in a maximum of four shades of grey.

The Gameboy's screen — like any other representational device — asks a formal question: how can you create a space through which a viewer can imaginatively move with such strict technical limitations. The solution to this problem is a drastic reduction of objects to symbols: waves are uniform stripes of grey and white, all trees are the same tree, and all buildings are the same façade stretched or contracted to give a sense of variety but never quite to the point where they could logically contain their single room interiors (which, anyway, are stored on another map so to walk through a doorway is to teleport into a parallel dimension). The glyph you pour yourself into as you play no more resembles yourself than a drawing of a landscape resembles the hand that made it.

And yet, despite this shonky, cut and pasted, bastardised attempt at depth, this environment is, for me, as deeply invested with emotional memory as the house where I grew up or the literal streets I played in as a child. There is something uncanny about seeing its textures and shapes dismembered and reconstituted as an impossible parody of itself, like when you dream of returning to a house you haven't visited for years to find its rooms are not where you left them. And something disillusioning too: you are confronted with the fact that what you took for a possible reality was only a collection of signifying units whose meaning was dependent on your imaginative participation, your willingness to believe them.

§

I needed a cigarette, and so I stepped out onto the street and tried to fold myself into the space beneath the concrete lip of a doorway where the water gathered like stalactites. I could have gone to the yard out the back and sheltered beneath an awning in the warm glow of a filament lamp, but, on that day, it didn't seem worth it in the calculus of risk that all queer people (but not only queer people) do as we move through the world. I thought to myself *I'm used to this. I am as much at home in a fractured maze of visible & invisible walls as anywhere. I've learned what every little queer must learn: to be alert, to be aware of where you are & are not safe.* And there was half of me that was ashamed for thinking this, for standing in the rain.

By then Bradbury Place was doing its best impression of a river, wide and flat and not far off the point where it empties into the sea and gives up its name. To my right, I could just about see the southern end of Sandy Row, one of those gaps in my mental cartography of the city, where I rarely go and if I were to venture into I would affect a name less revealing of my background and try to minimise the outward signs of my queerness. In my mind, I swept over the West of the city, where the euphemistic 'peace walls' translate the conceptual fragmentation of Belfast into physical truth, and was reminded that the streets through which I move were, until recently, the ground of a diffuse and lengthy war (which has not resolved as such, but metastasised into a purely symbolic conflict), and, because of the intractable presence of as yet unrecovered bodies, remains an unconsecrated and unbounded cemetery.

IV

(Still Lifes)

A GRAPEFRUIT

Because it cannot scream
it fills the room with fragrance.
It cannot help itself

but be so round, so pink,
so full of acid & vitamins
& sugar so far beneath them

it hits the tongue as lack.
It tastes like punishment.
What more could I want?

PAVLOVA

It has such ease; it holds
its shape like a cat: bonelessly

relaxed. Do I resent it? Its gloss.
How it resists the whip

by loving it. To spread
is to begin negotiations;

it clings to the spoon
like history.

It goes coral-hard in the oven
& waits for morning

when I'll pick it up & tap
its base & judge it.

Sometimes I think the fact
that I am still alive

is a sign of my own
lack of conviction.

THE MEAT-SHAPED STONE

is exactly what you'd
imagine: a one-inch cube
of jasper impersonating
a bite-size lump of
pork. At first it's the
top that fascinates: the
thin innumerable sheets
of stone laid down at a
rate of centuries, then
cut & glazed brick-red
to imitate the fat as it
begins to lose opacity, &
cracks. But take another
look & you'll notice
the erratic notches
hacked out of the lower
half; its colour which
hovers somewhere un-
translatable between
brown & pink. I know
that if I licked this stone
in search of salt & oil or
bit down expecting the
soft resistance of well-
cooked pig, I would be
disappointed. I don't
know if that would stop
me.

STUDY OF A TOMATO

Imagine it, substantial as a planet
& twice as red. Begin with this.

Establish an outline, round
as ontology, but solid, filled

with as much tomato as it can hold.
It has no bones, no beak, no claws.

Its form is soft & softer.
It is mostly juice, which is not blood

& not unlike it. It has & is —
like everything — a body.

Let's open it. Here is the pulp
in which your tongue might read

the season's rainfall
& map the land it fell upon,

here are the seeds
to which it's so devoted,

& here is that little green nipple
(you've likely, by now, plucked out)

which implies the vine
& all its red brethren.

It does not speak. It is not
a symbol for menstruation

or the absence thereof.
This is this & only this.

Pomegranate

Like nothing so much as a pomegranate, the pomegranate hangs between a cabbage & a squash, until, that is, a bullet enters from the right & opens it. It splits like a mouth stretched beyond the limit of its jaw. Its soft hold on the bullet as it passes through is enough to drag the fruit to the left. Its lower half is hanging from the thinnest flap of skin. At the apex of its swing, it twists as if to hide its open flank & almost manages to pull itself together as the string realises it has given all the give it has & jerks the pomegranate back towards the space it just vacated.

The cloud of juice & pips it spat the moment the bullet entered has thinned to a few specks drifting into ever looser arrangements. It dribbles some red juice from the spout its base has now become. But even this runs dry. The pomegranate has sprayed so much of itself into the air, it's hard to say whether this purse of skin can be called a pomegranate at all, or if the

word came spinning with the
last few gobs of flesh through
the space where the cabbage
still hangs plumb & the squash
still rests on the concrete & the
cucumber I haven't mentioned
yet still goes unmentioned.

On Reflection

The focus of the lens is
balanced like a Jesus bug on
the surface of a mirror, & not
on the flowers that it contains.
The flowers are silk, cut &
folded to perform the role of
flowers (& not just any flowers,
but those painted by the lesser
elder Brueghel). A current runs
through the tempered, perfect
glass & fractures it. The cracks
happen & happen everywhere
at once. They come from no
particular direction. They
do not spread like a net, nor
emanate like lace. The image
sets to rippling. It blurs like
alcohol on paint. The serrated
chunks of glass begin to fall &
as they make their progress to
the bottom of the frame, we see
a fraction of the subject they
contained pass through them,
& shrug off their holding.

Falling Bird

It's nice to meet you pheasant, says
the pheasant, or he would if he
were not stone-dead with his
two feet tied together by a string,
which, out of shot, is cut so the
bird falls, incrementally, the arrow
of his beak made literal, the cursive
ascender of his tail describing
his angle of approach towards
his fainter double, who rises in
a pool of water, or, to be exact,
on its meniscus, which is, as yet,
unbroken & has not thrown itself
in a ragged, partial cone around
the point where the bird meets
himself, face first.

*Don't we look exactly like a pair of
pheasants?* he might say, *Doesn't our
motley of blues & golds look painted
on with oils & shine so beautifully
against the dusky grapes, the rough
brown plaster of the wall? There is a
chance I love you.*

FIDELITY

Does it bother the apple
that these teeth now cutting
through its pale green flesh
were, not so long ago, pressed
into my earlobe with just
enough force to bring the blood
to the skin but no further?
Does the apple mind
that the lips on which its juice
is smeared still faintly taste
of my cum? Would
the apple be concerned
if I said it was not an apple,
but a quince, a plum,
an apricot, or a fiction;
if the mouth now grinding it
were not a mouth but
a space I've shaped to hold
the desire I've nowhere else
to put but here, right here?

A PUMPKIN

With effort I get the knife in, & with
a little hinging of the wrist, I split
the fruit along a shallow runnel
where its shape suggests it wants to split.
It exposes its creamy interior.
Its flesh, like all flesh, is a distraction;
it wraps around an orange mess
of filaments. I scoop this out, I pull
each pale seed from its entanglement.
& because I want a violence
more intimate, I do this with my hands
& feel its wet potential turn to pulp
beneath my nails. By now the fruit
is more the absence of itself:
an orange cup enclosing what it's lost.
There are many things I should confess.
To begin with: this vicious sympathy,
this want (& inability) to know
how it feels to hold a space
at the centre oneself, & have it filled;
to bend the self around the presence
of something not-quite-other, not-quite-I;
to give the body up as nourishment.
I cut the pumpkin's two bright domes
to crescent moons. I do this in the hope
that when the resurrection comes,
everything I have subjected thus
will be returned inviolate
& I'll be nothing & forgiven.

v

(Landscapes)